Rocking

A selection of **On the Green** pieces

first published in *The Arran Voice*

Written and illustrated by
Alison Prince

ISBN 978-0-9564474-0-1

Acknowledgement is made to *The Arran Voice*, where the original form of the pieces in this book first appeared

Typeset and designed by Margo Wheeler

Printed at Clydeside Press,
37 High Street, Glasgow G1 1LX

Published by Voice for Arran
Burnfoot, Whiting Bay, Isle of Arran, KA27 8QL
info@voiceforarran.com

Contents

Mary Anne and Mr Dyson

Mary Ann lived in the cupboard under the stairs, together with the Ronuk furniture polish and two hollow elephants made of black pottery that were supposed to have hyacinths planted in their howdahs when spring came. She looked like a brown pig with no legs, and she was our vacuum cleaner. As a small child, I was very scared of the loud noise she made – and of the knobs on the side of her head end that might have been eyes or ears. Or possibly both.

Periodically my mother would unscrew one of these knobs and pull out a long, wobbly spring that had the stub end of what looked like black chalk on the end. When I came across conte crayon as an art student years later, I was immediately reminded of Mary Ann. At the time, though, I just watched in slightly horrified fascination as my mother fitted a new, much longer black chalk on each spring, then screwed them back in. "Carbon brushes," she explained.

Did she really know what they were? I'm not sure. She was very proud of her education at the Harris Academy, but it seemed to have concentrated mostly on Sir Walter Scott. In Physics at my school, we were told sternly about armature winding and conductivity, and I had one of those *Oh, I see* moments. Not that it stayed in my unscientific brain for long. I still have to think about water going fast through narrow pipes and slowly through wider ones before I can get my head round amps and volts.

The tendency to visualise everything doesn't fit well with theory. People used talk about cars having horse-power, and that was fine. Our Ford 10 was as strong as ten horses. Quite how they all fitted under the bonnet was another matter, but I knew by then that this was a silly idea, so I didn't say anything about it. Learning that you mustn't be silly is one of the saddest lessons of childhood.

Technology has of course galloped on, whether or not it has legs. It's gone well beyond Mary Ann in its aim to be lighter and less substantial. I mean, just look at the Dyson. Mary Ann used to gobble and groan her way around the house until she was full, then she let you take her bottom end off and empty her bag (do excuse me, I don't wish to sound gynaecological about this, but she was somehow undeniably female.) The Dyson, on the other hand, is a Cloud Nine hermaphrodite, transparent round the middle, hiding its pipe inside its hose, willing to be whatever you want. It's a stick insect of a cleaner, a juggler's trick kept going by the sheer imagination of its inventor – and of course by the brightly-coloured plastic that embodies it.

Sexless though it may be, my Dyson has a certain personality. Perhaps because it is purple and yellow, it suffers from schizophrenia, veering between being a rapacious banker on one hand and a fainting Victorian lady on the other. It will swallow a silk scarf out of sheer greed then have an attack of the vapours that call for smelling salts and a screwdriver. Mary Ann would just have said, "Sorry, M'm," and wait for you to retrieve it from her inner parts, but the Yellow Peril requires a tracheotomy and a lot of fiddling about with a piece of wire.

That's nothing compared with the major surgery required to deal with a broken drive belt. The patient has to be laid on the kitchen table, ideally with a nurse at hand to mop the surgeon's brow and hand the screwdriver, pliers and scissors. *Scissors?* Well, yes. Almost inevitably, there will be thread, string or a trailing bit from the Moroccan rug entwined round the brush bar. It's like Charlie Chaplin eating his bootlaces, only a lot less funny. But with any luck, you get the patient screwed up again and good for a bit more potentially collapsing service.

I blame the Chinese. They are the traditional masters of frail technology. I once took the top off a permanently-running loo in a Beijing hotel because the noise was driving me bats, and found that the mechanism consisted of a sponge, a bit of wire and a small plastic lotus petal. I'm not kidding. But at least it could be mended by bending the wire. I don't think the Chinese had spanners then.

Neither do I, except for the grid in the shower outlet when it clogs up. Everything else quivers like a nervous greyhound. My first computer had a mouse that died periodically and required cardiac arrest treatment. The current one has a love-hate relationship with Outlook Express. I ignore all complaints, which are clearly designed to keep cyber-neuro-surgeons in business. One of these days, all Western babies will have an electrode implanted under the scalp at birth and be on hifi for life. Come back, Mary Ann. All is forgiven.

Power Point Sleep

Bright wakefulness at four in the morning tends to make you wish you were asleep, unless you are at a very good party. But the more you long for it, the more inaccessible it gets. You begin to think about sleep deprivation as a form of torture, yet the thought of getting up and mooching around in a sleeping house is deeply unattractive. Nearly as bad, though, is being overwhelmed by a desire to be asleep when you ought to be awake. Has anyone else ever been overwhelmed by a wave of threatened unconsciousness when someone is giving a talk or a committee is debating the details of its latest failed efforts to raise funds? My own, utterly infallible nemesis is the PowerPoint presentation.

Show me a laptop and a screen, switch on the home page with the patch of click boxes in the bottom right-hand corner and I've gone. Unconsciousness blacks me out like a general anaesthetic. I know why, of course. It's the only way to duck being bombarded by bullet-pointed facts that the speaker Also Reads Out To You in case you are blind, dyslexic or a congenital idiot. My mind does an instant runner. The presenter should be grateful for the apparent discourtesy. It spares him or her from a highly confrontational experience.

I think this automatic escape started when I was a student. Art History lectures were given on Fridays at five o'clock by an eminent professor who spoke extremely slowly in a heavy Teutonic accent. We went to sleep like litters of puppies, heads on each other's shoulders. He didn't notice as far as I knew – but then, I only woke up when the silence began. Luckily, he'd written a hefty book, chunks of which formed the substance of his lectures, so it was no problem to mug the stuff up while conscious and somewhere else. Ever since, I've regarded all external phenomena as optional rather than compulsory. The slightest whiff of boredom results in cop-out. And blackout.

But waking in the night seems to be the exact converse. The brain has found it is interested in something, so it starts hopping about like a toddler in a cot who's decided that morning has come. It tries to do Sudoku with letters instead of numbers or it plays a tune to the end and you think, 'Don't start again!' But it does start again. And again, and again.

Then there are the plans and the lists. Mostly these are about stuff you've already put in the mental Pending file. *Make up spare bed, cut out last year's blackberry branches, write the bit about Anne Boleyn's execution, phone the Arts Council, write to the Guardian.* Is any of this worth waking up for? No.

Everyone has advice to offer on insomnia. The truly Spartan tell you to get up, have a hot drink, then clean your teeth and go to bed all over again. But I'm not *that* awake. It's just that I'm not asleep, either. Some advise a soothing hot bath, lavender oil on your pillow, a dream-catcher on your wall. Too late. They should have been done before, and I don't believe in them anyway.

When all else fails, I read. It's very enjoyable, but three hours of someone else's words in the middle of the night tends to leave you feeling wrecked the next day. And sometimes the thought of switching the light on, fishing for a book, groping for the glasses and getting the eyes focussed on lines of print is too exhausting to contemplate. Back to the drawing board – surely there must be some technique of managing the wayward mind?

My daughter says airily, 'It's quite simple – you just breathe out more than you breathe in. You're asleep in two minutes.' It works for her, I've seen her do it. She goes off to sleep like someone stepping on an escalator, carried away into the depths of unconsciousness with no effort. And I'm left standing at the top.

At 4.30 this morning, I had a truly brilliant idea. If boredom induces sleep during the day, then boredom at night should do the same thing. Now – this is a dreadful confession – I've always thought meditation was seriously boring. If I made a space between thoughts as told, it was very pleasant, but if the space got any bigger, I simply went to sleep. I woke once to find the rest of the Yoga class giggling because I'd been snoring. There was something about that oh-so-calm voice asking us to think about our toes. Each individual toe. Then our feet. *Be aware of any tension in them and release it. Now think of the ankles … now the calves …* and I'd usually gone. Sometimes I'd get as far as the knees, but I never knew what happened after that.

So I thought about my feet at half past four. Pleasantly warm. Soles tingling a bit. Boring. *Must make up the spare* – Hush. Feet. Feet ….

And then it was morning.

Bukowski's Cat

A friend has sent me a poem by Charles Bukowski called *Startled into life like fire*. I still have it propped beside the computer. Bukowski was an American Beat poet, much given to debauchery of all kinds, and yet in writing about his cat, he touches on a lovely bit of simplicity. The poem is written without capitals or punctuation, and the middle sections go like this:

he is alive and plush and final as a plum tree

neither of us understands cathedrals or the man outside watering his lawn

if I were all the man that he is cat – if there were men like this the world could begin.

After reading it slowly a couple of times, it settled in as a chunk of real truth. That's what the Beat generation was about, of course – embracing truth the way it is. Bukowski was born in 1920 and died in 1994, and the notion of spin and the keeping up of appearance was still in its infancy. There's always been fashion, but I can't imagine him perusing the subtle supplements that slide out of Sunday newspapers, anxious to know exactly what he should eat and wear, and whether he was admiring the correct people. He wrote a fair amount of wild stuff, but when it came to the cat, he just said what he perceived to be true.

As all cat owners know, the feline psyche understands fear and pleasure, but it has no truck with pretence, no feeling of obligation and no guilt. If a cat comes to you and curls up in your lap, it's simply because it wants to. When it jumps off and does something else, it's no good you trying to persuade it to come back and go on cuddling. Non-cat people find this intensely annoying. They accuse the species of cupboard love. Recent press reports cited a paranoid piece of 'research' that held cats to be capable of actual manipulation. Somebody claimed to have proved that cats make a sound similar to that of a human baby *because they reckon* that's the best way to stir the owner into reaching for the tin-opener. How mad is that? Cats do not go in for abstract reckoning. Their motives are concrete ones and their understanding of how humans think is more or less zilch. They do what they do and with any luck we get the message. Rubbing round the owner's legs when hungry is a straightforward request. The cat isn't pretending to love anyone, it's simply saying *Please feed me.* Or more likely, *Feed me.* I'm not sure that 'please' is in the cat vocabulary.

Dogs are a different kettle of psychology altogether. As pack animals, they have a desperate underlying need for someone to tell them what to do. Unless the owner fulfils this need, Fido will shred the house and behave like a football hooligan until someone takes charge of him. This, of course, is worrying to the cat person, because many humans show signs of being the same. Large numbers of them grab any opportunity to indulge in a rampage once they are let off the lead. Look at the office party. Look at Buchanan Street on a Saturday night. Look, in fact, at football hooligans. Generally speaking, you can't put a cat on a lead (except for the odd, deeply eccentric Burmese), so they have no concept of being off it. Or, as the doggy lot claim, no concept of loyalty.

Is loyalty a virtue or a personal necessity? Now, there's a

radioactive question, pulsing with implications. For dogs, it's a built-in factor. If they haven't a leader to be loyal to, they're in a mess. Human leaders assume the same thing to be true. Governments strive to earn (or more commonly, command) the loyalty of the populace. But around half the populace consists of cat-type people who don't see why they should be loyal to anyone and certainly don't want to be put on a lead. Hence the deep unpopularity of all measures designed to make them safer and more efficient. Cats are not interested in being safe. They take colossal risks all the time. Some of them learn that roads are populated with cars that can squash them, but others can't or won't. You have to respect a cat for that, even while in tears as you dig a hole to bury it.

It's not easy to imagine a country run by cats. Getting them to join a political party other than the Greens would be tricky to start with. They'd never attend conferences at which the Top Cat outlines plans to which they must all adhere. Working their way up the hierarchy with the proper degree of sensitive cunning is a skill that no cat possesses. They are much more likely to snipe from their own tree-top and write letters to the Guardian (a cat paper if ever there was.)

If there were men like this the world could begin …

Such a lovely idea. But, were men like that in charge, the problems of getting them to agree might be, as the phrase goes, like herding cats. Sadly and un-poetically, we probably need the dog-people to do the governing bit. And that's enough to make a cat laugh.

Bah to Begonias

I cannot love begonias. This will send shudders of horror through their Appreciation Society – there's bound to be one – but I don't care. These plants look to me as if they're out on a perpetual stag night, red-faced and roaring with vulgar laughter, slapping each other on the back. Their defenders will no doubt fire off indignant e-mails, claiming that many forms of their beloved plant are models of tasteful discretion. They may be right, but evaluation of modesty depends on where you're coming from. A Mother Superior will not judge it in quite the same way as the Madame of a menage.

Being past the age when either of these callings seems feasible, I tend more to the Independent Dinosaur view – hopelessly out of date and with a cranky respect for the original way of things. To me, begonias look as if they've been manufactured rather than grown. Those outrageous great leaves, mottled in red and orange on the end of beetroot-coloured stalks, and the explosive flowers in violent colours must have been produced by a design studio somewhere. Probably in Dubai, which holds the crown for international vulgarity, in between turning out plastic palm trees and computer pop-ups.

Prejudices, of course, are never logical. Anyone professing to dislike all things garish ought to object to parrots, for instance, but they tick my boxes, no problem. Their sharpness of shape justifies them, not to speak of the mordant humour that lurks in the eye. And those huge red poppies that bloom a metre high amid their hairy green leaves, though absolutely day-glo, look wonderful against a background of shadowed greenery. They have a kind of clarity, being an empty hollow with a black, powdery centre, open to moths and to any casual viewer. Poppies are simple and honest. There is an element of poetry about them, too, I suppose because of their elegiac evoking of the First World War battlefields. Can you imagine a begonia so gracefully bearing that emotional message? No hope. Too lumping and pretentious by far.

There are two begonias in my greenhouse. This is somewhat embarrassing after what I've just said, but they arrived free a couple of years ago with a lot of fritillaries from a mail-order firm. They were crumpled-looking corms and I felt sorry for them, the way you do for dogs with wrinkly faces. (May as well upset the Kennel Club while I'm at it.) So I potted them up and hoped they wouldn't grow into anything too nasty. They were embarrassingly grateful. They thrust out rapid shoots that put on an inch or more a day, then grew fat buds that within a very few days had burst into a fantasia of salmon-red blossoms. To their credit, they are not the sort that looks like beetroot salad. Their flowers are quite delicate, with pointed petals. Apart from their aggressive colour, they are reasonably discreet, except for their red-nosed chirpiness and their tendency to interfere with the cucumbers. I'm kind of touched by them. They clearly love their greenhouse. Every winter they lie doggo and I wonder half-hopefully if they've died in their sleep, but come April, all they need is the most accidental sprinkle of water and they're off again, like a concert-party on the Pier. No, not Brodick Pier, don't be silly. Can you imagine? Fish-net stockings, top-hats, 'Hello, hello, who's your lady friend?' It might have some appeal to the Tourist Board, but CalMac would probably regard it 'inappropriate.' There is absolutely no touch of the begonia about CalMac.

Let's face it, there are worse things than a bit of vulgarity. What about bracken, for goodness' sake? That goes well beyond rudeness, it is the total barbarian army. Have you driven over the Ross lately? There used to be a stunning view down the glen, but all you can see now is an ocean of dull, green bracken, harbouring ticks like a biological weapon. The dinosaur in me starts bellowing. When the cattle used to roam free, they trampled this noxious growth down and you could see the shape of the hill, with its changing seasonal colours due to heather and whin and thyme. Now, this dreadful army has taken over. You can't walk through it and nothing else can grow in its company. It is in my view a worse nuisance than Japanese knotweed.

On a trip to the Scilly Isles, I noticed that farmers were taking flail-cutters to their bracken. "We need to keep on top of it," one of them told me. "Otherwise it chokes everything." Here on Arran, we're not on top of it. Quite the reverse – it's on top of us. In my dog-walking days, I used to do a lot of bracken-trampling. It works very well, specially if done in the spring, and it's free, unlike the modern tactic of spraying it with noxious chemicals. What about some bracken-stamping parties next spring? Accompanied by a bottle of white wine and some tomato sandwiches, it could be quite fun. But something needs to be done. In fact, come to think of it, I'd prefer to have the hillsides covered in begonias. Come back, my vulgar friends. All – or at least, quite a lot – is forgiven.

The Poet and the Sheep

Looking out of the window, I can see white breakers galloping along the horizon, and the bare trees are thrashing about in the wind. Bad news for the boat, and there probably won't be any post again, but I don't care. We're past Christmas. The days have stopped their awful shrinking into darkness. We're on the long roll towards summer, and whatever the sky chooses to chuck down at us in the next couple of months, the light will go on growing and the shoots of spring bulbs are poking through the earth. Things are all right.

Meanwhile, Arran goes on throwing up wee bits of bizarre event that keep the days unpredictable and funny. About to drive down to the pier the other day to meet a pal off the boat, I was brought up short by the arrival of a poetry-writing friend on the doorstep. He beamed in his affable way and was quite unfazed when I said I had to go out. 'That's fine,' he said. 'Be great if you could give me a lift to Kings Cross, though.' He is the kind of poet who hitch-hikes.

On our way along the road he read me a poem. 'It was written by me and my partner,' he said, 'while walking on Arran.' Peering through the rain and doing my best to dodge the potholes, I tried to listen with suitable attention. Words seemed to get chewed up by the windscreen wipers – or maybe I just wasn't attending properly. I kept thinking how clever it was to write a poem with someone else while striding across a moor. It's as much as I can do to put a few lines together in dead silence on my own. Anyway, the poet got out at the Kings Cross road, leaving the paper with the poem on it sliding around on the front seat, and I went on along the windy Heights and down the hill to Lamlash.

At the Dyemills corner there was a Blackface ewe grazing calmly on the patch of grass before the bridge. She glanced up, munching, looking preoccupied and busy, the way sheep do, and took another mouthful. But would she think the grass on the other side of the road was nicer? Visions of crashed cars and newly-dead mutton flashed through my mind, so I turned into the police station where wonderful Jim took charge of the situation with instant efficiency. I drove on wondering if he had a couple of police sheep dogs waiting patiently for a copper with a crook (the shepherd kind I mean, not a burglar, that would have been very unproductive), but had to accept that he'd probably just phone the farmer.

All the same, it had been somehow pleasing to get delayed by a poet and a sheep. If I could wish for anything in this New Year, it's for an increase in gentle eccentricity. Not full-blown idiocy, you understand – there's far too much of that around already, specially among organisations that should know better. The boring insanity of officialdom is about as amusing as woodworm in your piano legs. No, what I'm after is mild, individual persistence in doing whatever seems most attractive at the moment, regardless of what the general standards of correctness may be. And speaking of those, I've just had a New Year e-mail greeting that cocks a splendid snook at all toeing of the line. I reproduce it here in case you'd like to stick it on the office wall. Or for individuals, somewhere more intimate.

'Please accept with no obligation, implied or implicit, my very best wishes for an environmentally conscious, socially responsible, low stress, non-addictive, gender neutral celebration of the winter solstice holiday, and/or adjacent days, practised within the most enjoyable traditions of the religious persuasion or of course the secular practices of your choice, with respect for the religious or secular traditions of others, or their choice not to practice religious or secular traditions at all, no criticism implied by that provision.'

It gets worse as it goes on.

'May you have a financially successful, personally fulfilling, and medically uncomplicated recognition of the onset of the conventionally accepted calendar year, but not without due respect for former calendars or the calendars of choice of other cultures whose contributions to society have helped to make the World great, and without regard to the race, ethnic origin, age, physical ability, religious faith, political belief, choice of computer platform, car ownership or sexual preference of the wishee.'

That lot has brought my computer out in an explosion of wiggly green underlining. Pcs are nothing if not pc – nobody's found out how to programme in a sense of humour. And do not mention those horrible smileys.

Discarding such irritations, I wish all friends, sheep, poets and readers a very happy year to come. But I must draw your attention to the following:

'Without prejudice to the informality of any relationship, business or social, it must be pointed out that by accepting this greeting you are accepting these terms.' Be warned

Press Grey Button

A strange little object turned up in the post a few days before Christmas. Admittedly, it's a time when strange objects tend to arrive unbidden, but this one wasn't a present. It came as an apology from a mail order firm who had failed to send something destined to be a present for someone else. You know how it is at Christmas. Anyway, this small thing looked like a TV screen for a dolls' house – the size of a matchbox but flatter, with no visible controls except for a single grey button. It was on a wide hook, suggesting that it could be worn in some way, possibly to announce your name to anyone interested, in case you have happened to forget it. I turned it over a couple of times, feeling like a monkey with a new and baffling form of peanut, and handed it to my daughter Sam, who is good at things with screens. 'What's this?'

'It's a pedometer,' she said without a moment's hesitation. 'You hook it on your belt.'

'How do you know?'

'It says. Look, there are instructions.'

Sure enough, a small and much-folded piece of paper had been inserted under the hook of the minuscule screen. And yes, it said, *Personal pedometer*. I was tempted to wonder if there was such a thing as an *im*personal pedometer, but these philosophical questions tend to hold things up if you simply want information. So I kept going with the leaflet. *Clip the pedometer on your belt or waistband, about 14mm from the centre. Press grey button to start.*

'I want to try,' said Sam's daughter, Letty. 'What does it do?'

'It counts the number of steps you take.'

For the next half hour, we were subjected to an endlessly stepping eleven-year-old, marching on the spot whenever she stopped, head screwed to one side, to look at the numbers changing on the tiny screen. Then she'd be off again. Busy counting and checking, she trod on the cats from time to time and collided with various things, but hardly noticed. We got frequent reports. 'I've done four hundred and thirty-five!' 'I've done six hundred and eighty!' Then she asked, "How many are you supposed to do?'

I was dreading that question, having read somewhere that you are going to drop dead of idleness if you fail to reach an Olympic target set by a sadist, but Sam had no such inhibitions. 'Ten thousand a day,' she said firmly.

Letty gawped. 'Ten *thousand!* Wow! You'd have to be walking all day!'

My feelings exactly.

Next time she checked, Letty found the little screen had gone blank because she'd accidentally pressed the grey button. 'Oh, stupid thing!' she said, and tossed it away like a cracker motto. Sam said, 'I might be quite interested to give it a go if you don't want it.'

I said she was more than welcome, but the thing then disappeared into the general Christmas state of Too Much. I didn't find it until mid-January, under a bed together with some wrapping paper and a lot of those silver wisps that fall off the tree faster than you can hang them on. And – I blush to admit this – I clipped the pedometer on my waistband and tried to kid myself I wasn't walking up and down stairs in order to impress it. By the time I'd put the washing out, I was up to 673 steps. It didn't seem much. I did some tai chi, but the miserable wee screen ignored that completely. It works by recording jolts, and tai chi is supposed to be smooth and non-jolty. It occurred to me that the self-deceiving step-counter could clock up an impressive score by sitting in an armchair and jiggling the pedometer with one finger. Four miles an hour while you're reading a life-style magazine with your feet up. How's that for a seductive thought?

I resisted it. Walking down to the village would clock up lots of steps. I checked the wee screen before I set out – and it was blank. Must have touched the grey button. Rats. I wrote *700* on a bit of paper to add to the total (surely I must have done 27 steps since putting the washing out?) and stumped off to the village. A friend offered me a lift on the way back, and I accepted. After all, they say one should not plunge into strenuous exercise too precipitately. The wee screen said a mere 1,630 when I got back. I took it off and sent it to Sam.

No, I have not been counting every step in my head ever since. But I've kept on walking to the village, at least when the sun shines. I'm making no promises if it rains. Life is too interesting and unpredictable to be dominated by a grey button. Specially one so mean-minded that it switches itself off.

Stickies

Chatting to my brother on the phone the other night, the conversation turned to Blu-tack. Something to do with his print of Breughel's *Hunters in the Snow* peeling off the wall, as far as I remember. But anyway, I told him they've invented White-tack now, and he was considerably startled, not being one for keeping up with modern trends. We agreed that Red-tack might be a mistake. Tacks of whatever colour tend to leave spots on the wall when you take the stuck thing off, and nobody wants the office looking as if there's been some kind of massacre. The police might declare it an Incident Zone and turf everyone out to stand in the street.

Following this, musing on adhesives kind of stuck in my mind, if you'll forgive the expression. The truth is, I have a deep-seated and constantly renewed detestation of the lot of them. If I try to stick anything papery, something will always be in the wrong place. If I stick a handle on a jug, it falls off, usually when full of daffodils or hot milk. My loathing of all things sticky started at school, when a fierce history mistress who was probably trying to be friendly handed me a tiny box that should have held matches. It had a picture of a Spanish galleon on the front, and my heart sank at the sight of it. She said, 'You're artistic – you might like to put this together.'

Inside were countless minuscule cardboard galleon

components, so small that you could only pick them up with tweezers. The diagram, once unfolded, measured about 3 inches square. And the whole thing required glue. The only kind of glue in our house was Seccotine, which came in a small tube with a pin in its nozzle to stop it leaking over everything else in the little-used box of Useful Stuff that lived in the cupboard under the stairs.

It has to be explained, we were not a handy family. My father played the piano and read Goethe and barely knew which end of a screwdriver was which. My mother claimed to be practical, but tended to fall at the first fence when her expertise was called on. She looked at the bits of galleon spread on the kitchen table and said, 'You need to take them in order.'

Have you ever noticed how irritating it is when people give you advice rather than actually helping? She didn't even get the stuck pin out of the Seccotine, just suggested putting it under boiling water. So much for Health and Safety, but they hadn't invented it then. After a struggle, I got the pin out with the tweezers from the medical box. They somehow got bent in the process. I managed to conceal this fact, but there was an awful row when they were next needed for removal of a splinter. And the blasted Seccotine didn't stick.

'It will if you hold the bits together,' my mother advised. So I sat there holding a microscopic mizzen mast and sail together for ages. When I tried to let go, my finger and thumb were stuck together. Pulling them apart was quite painful, and the mizzen mast was on my thumb and the sail was on my finger. Both bits had gone brown and transparent because of the Seccotine. With the courage of Nelson, I turned to the hull and managed to get some of its tiny components to unite, but it looked so untidy as to be rather disgusting, like a trodden-on cockroach. My mother had gone to listen to the Brains Trust with her knitting. When she came back after what seemed hours and said, 'Cocoa', I burst into tears. She scooped the bits of galleon back into their matchbox, supervised the cocoa-drinking in front of the fire in the sitting room – the kitchen had been really chilly – and packed me off to bed.

All the way to school the next morning, I felt sick at the thought of admitting my failure to the history mistress. She was going to put me through the mincer. I had been selected for an extraordinary favour, and the privilege filled me with terrified respect. Objects of amusement were rare in those wartime years. Heaven only knew why she had picked me, whose scant artistic ability mostly ran to furtive cartoons of the less popular members of staff – but whatever the reason, I'd blown it.

'I'm terribly sorry,' I confessed, 'but it wouldn't stick.'

To my utter astonishment, she laughed. 'I couldn't have done it, either,' she said.

Things got a bit better when they invented Cow gum, which wasn't made from cows at all but was a kind of rubber solution that you could rub off and roll into slightly disgusting black lumps. And when studying bookbinding, I got to grips, rather literally, with skin glue. That *was* made of cow, or at least calf, and sat in the corner of the workshop, stinking gently over a burner to keep it hot and runny. Strangely, that worked extraordinarily well.

Nowadays, I don't use glue at all if I can possibly help it, apart from the tacks, Blu or White. Drawing pins will do. Or a staple gun. Or nails. And I have absolutely nothing whatever to do with models of any kind. Specially galleons.

Crosswords and Blink

Scientists, I read the other day, are interested in how people solve crosswords. It has dawned on them that the working out of such puzzles is not entirely a matter of logic. Direct, spontaneous perception has a lot to do with it as well. As all puzzlers know, the answer to a clue can elude you for hours, then suddenly be transparently obvious.

I've often wished I could be conscious of the actual moment when this different sense-making happens, but it's like wanting to note precisely what going to sleep is like. It's easy to know you're sleepy, because you are still just about awake. Relaxed, yes, almost dreaming – but the final instant of blackout can't happen while you are trying to observe its nature, because such detached observation is the very essence of being awake. Hence the agonising Catch-22 of insomnia.

Does the same thing apply to crosswords, or can one have an awareness of a mental shift towards a perception that's about to happen? Scientists until recently have rubbished that idea. Intuition, they held, belongs to the right-hand part of the brain, the creative, non-rational half. Nobody knows what it gets up to, so it can't be relied on and is generally pretty useless. I suspect that those who want to see the nation properly organised are trying hard to rule out right-brain activity. Being one of those things that is sometimes present and sometimes not, it doesn't lend itself to statistical evidence and obstinately refuses to fit into tests. Very frustrating to those who want all forms of human activity to be logged on spreadsheets, but vital for poets and puzzlers.

I'm sure one *can* predict moments of perception. At the very least, there are ways to make their occurrence more likely. You need a perky state of mind with plenty of things running through it but no pressing necessities. A good night's sleep helps, though sometimes a wild clarity comes when you are beyond all reasonable tiredness and halfway to dream. The trick is to let the mind range widely, making as many free connections as possible. Once this free-ranging starts, a hint of impending success can sometimes come capering into your mind, waving a bunch of paper flowers in daft excitement.

Crossword-wise, I find the answer almost always comes before the reason underlying it. Take, for instance, an irritating little poser in a recent Guardian puzzle. CAN'T ALFRED MAKE UP HIS MIND? it asked. Five letters. Inevitably, my thoughts went barking off after the various electric hares triggered by the setter. Alfred the Great, Alfred burned the cakes, Alfred was unready – no, that was Ethelred. Alf Garnett, Alfie – wasn't there a song about Alfie? Useless, all of it. Alfred, Lord Tennyson - not the sort to be indecisive. Anagrams? *Flared,* perhaps? All this rubbish went round and round in repetitive circles. I put the paper aside and went off to do something else.

On return, I took a fresh look at the crossword, feeling absolutely sure I was going to get the answer. It came to me at once that there was a poet called Alfred Noyes. Of course! No-yes. Yes/no. Couldn't make up his mind. The answer came in a complete response, the logical explanation afterwards. A gestalt ('whole') moment, as the Berlin school of thought had it a century ago. This stuff has a long history.

It's also very useful, as Malcolm Gladwell points out in his study of unexpected understanding called *Blink* (recently reissued in Penguin Classics). He says direct perception is produced by 'the adaptive unconscious', and insists that the fundamental skill is to know your own mind. Too often, we suppress a bit of instinctive response because people who claim to know better pooh-pooh it, and we don't want to risk looking silly. That's fatal for crossword solving – and, in my view, for understanding almost anything that lies outside the most crudely obvious.

Take literature, for instance. The best of it is never a matter of straight logical comprehension. I read *Alice in Wonderland* as soon as I could read at all, and hardly understood a word, yet the Red Queen's unpredictable furies and the wild poetry of the White Knight were a wonderful preparation for the mixed madnesses of the real world. I didn't grasp until I was grown-up how the books related to cards and to chess, but understanding that fact added nothing except a bolt-on bit of side interest.

Poetry is almost wholly about communicating things that are strong but inexplicable. Phrases like *Not waving but drowning* or *Do not go gentle into that good night* are part of the language and we know how they make us feel – but what do they actually *mean?* Hard to find the words, for the poet has already selected words that do the job perfectly. They spring from their own logic, which does do not stand on the shoulders of a more common one.

Hence the fascination of a well-set crossword. Blink and you've missed it.

The Exploding Septic Tank

As a foot-loose student, I once went off to traipse round Europe, as one does, for about six weeks in the summer. When I came back to my parents' house, it looked rather different. A huge pile of red clay had engulfed most of the long, downward-sloping garden, and where the small bit of flat lawn used to be there was a deep, muddy hole with two men in it.

The men were not permanently resident in the hole. They were merely excavating the remains of the shattered septic tank, which had blown up the previous week at four in the afternoon. There's an ominous ring about that phrase, I feel. *At four in the afternoon.* A bit like Federico Garcia Lorca's *Lament for the Death of a Bullfighter*, except that his fatal event happened at five. *A las cinco de la tarde …* Apocalyptic stuff.

My mother failed to interpret the explosion poetically. Stoicism was more her line, coupled with a conviction that someone should pay for this. 'I'd only just cleared the tea-things away,' she said, taking a grim-faced Scottish pleasure in a good disaster. 'We'd been sitting out there with Mrs Hopkins.' I had the feeling she was slightly disappointed that nobody ended up in hospital. My father retreated to the pub, muttering something about the Somme. He wasn't keen on mud.

It was all to do with bindweed, the men said. It had grown in and choked the pipes. We had never actually known that the septic tank was underneath the tea lawn. We weren't exactly cucumber-sandwich people, but the big bang would have mucked up the home-made gingerbread no end. But we'd never thought what might be under the grass. Why would we? Septic tanks were invisible. One did not have to be aware of their presence. Water came into the house through pipes under the earth somewhere, and it went out again through other pipes, plus a certain contribution which nice people did not talk about. My parents, having seen the new septic tank lowered into the muddy hole, seemed abashed. In fact, they went off the house after that, and started looking for somewhere more respectable. I think they felt the place had behaved rather badly. Septic tanks were supposed to be silent and efficient, permanently.

It's different now. We live in the era of the septic tank's revenge. After all these years of patiently digesting all contributions, it is protesting at its modern misuse. Having no Garcia Lorca to plead the case, it does this by producing a powerful smell. You're lucky if you haven't noticed it. Stand by any burn where there are houses further up, and it will drift into your consciousness. During a dry summer, you may find it quite difficult to ignore.

If septic tanks had a spokesperson – or spokestank, I suppose – they would no doubt complain of increasing ill-treatment. During my parents' time, nobody used anything more violent than soap for washing and cleaning purposes, plus an occasional shake of Vim. Fairy soap in the kitchen, Lux in the bathroom, (or carbolic for the less pretentious,) Rinso for washing clothes, and later a product called Dreft, which was supposed to be good for your woollens, though when washing machines arrived, it came lathering out of the top of them like something out of the *Barber of Seville*.

Then the new-fangled detergents burst upon us. TV advertising insisted that we must use Surf and Tide and Domestos, which killed all known germs – *thump* – dead. The result of all this chemical warfare was that septic tanks began to suffer from indigestion. Many of them died. Many remain dead.

A septic tank is not an inert storage unit. It's a living entity, rather like a cow. It digests anything put into it. That's to say, all contents are turned into water and manure – provided they are not toxic. Compost heaps do the same thing, unless you are stupid enough to put dose them with a bacterial killer such as detergent or anything containing bleach. A living septic tank will go on for years and years, never needing to be emptied. A dead one stinks, and the owner has to keep paying the man with the tanker to empty it. I find it hard to believe people do this. It's so easy to keep a septic tank functioning sweetly. All you have to do is stop chucking kill-off chemicals down it.

Ecover provides a range of harmless and effective products for washing, bathing and clearning. After a tentative start a decade or so back, they're accessible everywhere, and they work very well. Your septic tank will purr along for years on a diet of Ecover and you-know-what, and you'll never have to phone the Council for colonic irrigation.

But do keep an eye on the bindweed.

Luck Management

We make our own luck, research reveals. How's that for a strange newspaper headline? Can luck actually be researched? A book called *The Luck Factor* says it can. Written by a psychologist, Dr Richard Wiseman (good name for someone in that trade), it starts from the reasonable premise that lucky people have a better time of it than the unlucky. Then, with less success, the author tries to find out how they do it.

Wiseman conducted interviews and distributed lots of psychometric questionnaires, which presumably invited his subjects to put a cross in numbered boxes running from *Strongly Agree* to *Strongly Disagree* (smother a yawn.) The conclusions were hardly surprising.

Lucky people maximise their opportunities, he discovered – though that sounds more like hard work than luck. They go through life *expecting* to be lucky. If they have bad luck, they manage to turn it into good luck. And, he claims, they make effective decisions because they act on intuition and gut feelings.

Hang on a minute while I get my head round this. It sounds very much as though he's saying lucky people behave as though they're lucky because they *are* lucky. Is that any help to the millions who are not? His one piece of advice is that we need to use our intuition and gut feelings. I agree with that, being someone who does it all the time. It works well, on the whole. There have been some spectacular failures, which we won't go into, but that's not the point. *The Luck Factor* needs a lot more detail on the mechanics of how to be lucky. Trusting to intuition is fine in theory, as long as you *have* intuition. If you don't, you're stalled from the start. So how do you develop this delicate form of radar?

Schools are no help. They deal in certainties, with a weary nod towards 'creativity' on a Friday afternoon when everyone is too knackered to do anything else. On the whole, modern education is about replacing gut feeling with demonstrable fact. A couple of centuries back (which is not long in the total scheme of things) the skills of using non-certainty were much stronger and more common. There is overwhelming evidence of 'second sight' among people in the remote Highlands, who always seemed able to know when someone had died hundreds of miles away or when a far-travelling son was going to turn up after years of absence. With no telephones or post, such intuition really did have to be reliable. You'd look sick if you'd killed the calf because Hamish was going to come home and then he didn't. Maybe such mistakes occurred and have been left off the record with an embarrassed cough, but it worked often enough for the certified instances to build up quite impressively.

This suggests that there really is an invisible network of linked event, much more comprehensive than the Internet, but non-mechanical. It also raises the probability that all time is in existence right now, not just the present moment and the known past. Our notion of the future as a thing that is yet to come is founded on the fact that we are stuck with the limitation of our own sense of Now. Looking outside that fixed relationship, there is no reason why all the time in the world, both apparently behind us and in front, should not be all round us at every moment. What we call coincidence is a fleeting connection with it.

As long as you don't impose your own reason, such connections happen quite often. You miss a train and the delay causes you to come face-to face with your long-estranged husband whom you thought was in India. (Honest – it happened to my grandmother.) The driver who picks you up on an Alpine road is your mate's uncle from Australia. You can absolutely *know* that you're going to win a raffle, as I did with a Devon Rex rabbit when I was ten. I told my father we'd need a hutch and he laughed and said he'd build one. A ludicrous idea from a man who couldn't change a fuse, but he didn't believe me. So the rabbit had to live in a cabin trunk with P&O labels, with wire netting across the front.

The unknown is only unknown to human beings, not to itself. It knows perfectly well what it is doing. You only have to believe in it, and be open to its suggestions. It probably comprises that totality that we describe as God. Certainly, it demands that you have enough courage, or faith, to step into it with complete acceptance. That demands a setting aside of any arrogance, and it chimes extraordinarily well with the humility inherent in all religious beliefs. The narrow, calculated power-seekers do not achieve success through a sensitive relationship with luck (which they despise.) They are driven by convoluted chicanery. When it goes wrong, they don't know how to be happy, so continuing chicanery is supported with poor people's money, which is not only criminal but stupid. We walk through a constant pattern of wondrous surprise, and there is nothing better.

Life is the perfect Lucky Dip.

The Sex Life of Slugs

'You shouldn't kill slugs,' said a visitor, staring with disapproval at the beer trap beside my courgette plants. 'Don't you know they have a wonderful sex life? I saw them on a science programme. Madly erotic.'

So I felt guilty. I tried hard to see slugs as erotic, but it was difficult. The visitor had gone on about the way they twine round each other and exchange slime, but somehow it didn't convey much of a thrill. Call me old-fashioned, but I do feel that a sex object needs to have a head, preferably with a face on the front, and a limb or two, never mind the bits you can't reveal except on a nudist beach. The gelatinous frill that goes along a slug's lower edge may drive other slugs wild with passion, but somehow I can't find it appealing. And anyway, I *like* hating slugs.

I hate slow drivers as well, but maybe that's because they are somewhat slug-like, crawling along the road as if unaware that a rampaging predator is pursuing them in a fury-fuelled CRV with expletives bursting out of its exhaust pipe. Not, of course, that I abandon my impeccable driving behaviour. The heyday of impetuous response died long ago, when men skewered each other over a trifling insult and women had brawny arms bulging out of rolled-up sleeves and meaty fists that could lay a neighbour flat with a rolling pin. Nowadays, we have to be content with loathing slugs.

This year, I dealt them a pre-emptive blow by means of several million microscopic nematodes. They arrived by post, in a plastic-covered packet, and looked like brown sugar. Not demerara, the soft kind that used to be called 'pieces', though I've never known why. After I'd tipped them into gallons of water as instructed and sprinkled them on, I went back to the house like a satisfied Jack the Ripper (or Tipper). Job done. The next morning, something had eaten through the stems of all my young cucumber plants. I fished the nematode package out of the bin and read the instructions again. *Nematodes do not attack snails*, it said, as though this should be counted in their favour. And, in a totally illogical way, it does.

Snails don't look so – what can one call it? Sluggish, I suppose. There's a certain delicacy about way they retreat into their shells. They are rather beautiful and private, withdrawing into perfectly-designed houses at any sign of threat. Slugs, poor things, are hopelessly un-private. And so ugly. Or slugly. Prejudice against them is dreadful. Any day now, someone is going to form a charity called LoveSlug or GoodSlime. (Why do organisations cram words together with a capital in the middle? I'd like VisitScotland much better if it had a space.) Anyway, the nematodes were less scrupulous than their suppliers thought. A few days after the cucumber attack, empty shells started turning up under flowerpots and in the folds of old sacks. The living brown sugar had evidently found a way round the problem.

It didn't last, though. The summer turned out to be such a nightmare of snail attack, Hitchcock could have made a movie about it, had he still been around. Every morning has started with a greenhouse inspection, armed with trowel and bucket. Snails by the dozen have been relocated to the burn. Sorry, but this is true. I suspect they swim, anyway. Overnight, they probably emerged, wet and irritated, and made their way back to the greenhouse. Like those nature programmes about baby turtles, except the turtles are trying to get into the water, not out of it. Meanwhile, huge specimens of slug started appearing. The black, leathery ones that are about five inches long. They'd obviously had their summer of deliriously happy sex, and were now bent on laying thousands of eggs in my greenhouse, as a multiple time-bomb to explode next spring. I suppose that's natural.

Nature doesn't give a damn about whether humans are self-sufficient and healthy or whether we stuff ourselves to death on junk food. We are the weird, extraneous species that arrived in the middle of everything else, full of mad ideas and outrageous creativity. Nature is not impressed by our sonnets and towers and aeroplanes, our music and electronics. She ignores our good or bad intentions and is not the least bit interested in our greenhouses. She just waits, with an occasional rolling of the eyes or smothered expletive, for us to muddle ourselves off to wherever we came from. I'd always hoped she made us, but I'm not sure now. If she did, she's not going to start being motherly again until we stop thinking we know better than she does.

I should never have abandoned the beer traps because of what the visitor said. The slugs enjoyed the alfresco pubs, and they died drunk and happy, which is more than many of us can say. If a sudden end interrupted their rapturous sex-life, tough. Next spring, I'll be laying in the six-packs.

A Very Vocal Fridge

My fridge groans. The old one never used to, it just sat there manufacturing frost until its freezer compartment turned into an iceberg that threatened to push the wee door off its hinges. Sorting that out involved a very wet business of carrying wobbly trays of water to the sink without spilling them (impossible) and mopping up the kitchen floor afterwards. But the old fridge was a good soul, stoic, decently behaved and totally silent. It was second-hand when I bought it 23 years ago and its door had got a bit spotty, but I went over the rust patches with Tippex and you'd never have known. It's still going strong in the works canteen where it now lives.

Getting a new fridge wasn't mere frivolity – it was forced on me when the kitchen had a facelift, because the inspired friend who redesigned the whole thing changed all the built-in stuff round. That meant there wasn't space for the existing fridge and the small, separate freezer. 'Deep breath time,' he said. 'You need a fridge-freezer.' So I bought this all-in-one affair. It's quite modest, compared with some of the monsters on the market. I couldn't live with one of those wardrobe-sized American jobs that have iced water on tap and look as if you'll get a blast of Dolly Parton when you open the door. Mine is about the same height as I am, but a good bit wider. And it groans. It keeps up a gentle muttering and snoring the whole time, but periodically it says, 'Errrgggghhhhhh…' as if it's turning over in its sleep. At first I used to creep downstairs and peer nervously into the kitchen in case there was a burglar with a headache hiding behind the door, but I got used to it.

This strange machine was manufactured in Italy, which may have something to do with it. Italy is, after all, a famously musical nation, where one may see young men leaping onto café tables to belt out a Verdi aria in competition with each other – at least, they did back in my camping days. They probably just listen to i-pods now. But I do toy with the idea that Italian industry might produce fridge-freezers with baritone voices. They could do fan-heaters that are tenors as well, along with alto spin dryers and soprano whisks. Get them all going at once, and you'd have a kitchen choir. Hellish if they hadn't been tuned to the same key, though.

Away with such fantasies – the answer has to be more prosaic. Maybe the thing gets indigestion because it self-defrosts. This process is a mystery to me. Fridges make condensation, right? That's why the old kind iced up. But these new ones deal with their own ice. What I want to know is, *where does it go?* I've investigated the innards of the groaner, and note that there are dots of ice over its interior rear wall. There is also a small hole at the bottom of this wall, which puts one in mind of some kind of biological function – but then what? If water goes through that hole, does it turn into oxygen and hydrogen again? It's an alarming idea. Hydrogen is lighter than air, I seem to remember. If enough hydrogen fills the kitchen, will the whole place take off like one of those heart-shaped plastic balloons? It's a built-on bit, additional to the rest of the house, so it might. If this happens, I hope the cats will have the good sense to jump ship – I'd hate to think of them mewing their way across the Atlantic in an airborne kitchen.

Speaking of long journeys, when I came back from Australia the fridge was brain-dead. I'd left it more or less empty, but couldn't switch it off without switching the freezer off as well, which would have been curtains for the contents. Julie-whom-the-cats-love said worriedly, 'I put fresh milk in a couple of times, but it turned.' Right enough, the fridge was silent and its interior felt tepid. Its light was on, but it was utterly silent. Not the slightest mutter or snore, let alone a groan. It seemed to have had some kind of stroke.

My first line of defence in such crises is to do nothing and hope things get better on their own. It works fine for most illnesses and quite often for absence of money. Admittedly, it might not be so good in case of fire. But it might work for a catatonic fridge. Anyway, I bunged a lot of new foodstuff into the ex-groaner and went to see what the computer was up to. (Three thousand messages purporting to be undelivered e-mail notifications, since you ask.) After a bit the cats started complaining that they hadn't been fed for two whole hours, so I went down to the kitchen. And the fridge was groaning happily.

Inside, it was wonderfully cold. Beads of water were turning into ice on its back wall. I closed its door very gently, not to upset it, and patted its roof affectionately. All to do with the thermostat, I suppose. Lacking anything to cool, it had nothing to do and nothing to grumble about, so it nearly died. That's the nature of unemployment. Bit scary, really. Better keep busy, or else. Excuse me while I get on.

Reindeer at the Ready

What I need is a reindeer.
Or preferably several reindeer.
Flying ones. I've no intention
of keeping the real sort, which would be messy, smelly and peculiar.
Reindeer probably eat a special kind of moss that has to be gathered
before dawn while the frost is still on it. They'd get strange diseases
like harness galls and hoof-rot and spavins (I seem to remember those
from *Black Beauty*), and their horns would get jammed in the stable
door, always supposing I managed to build a stable. They'd drop dead
in the middle of Whiting Bay, causing people to miss the boat and/or
write letters to SEPA and the RSPRdr. It would turn out that I should
have had a reindeer permit from DEFRA , together with proof of the
required vaccinations, and a sledge-driving licence from Swansea.
Any surviving reindeer would get a parking ticket from the local fuzz.

Flying reindeer would be immune to all that. I don't know who
dreamed up the notion of Santa Claus whistling over the chimney
pots with his light-as-air team, but it is much to be desired. But I can't
imagine how reindeer can fly, with not so much as a wing between
them. Maybe they are jet-propelled by methane from all that special
moss. We're told that a single cow threatens the planet by producing
more greenhouse gas than fifteen mobile homes – but developing the
Arran flying cow might be tricky. Their weight-to-gas ratio doesn't
seem promising. And sheep would be no good. Once off the ground

they'd probably turn upside down, and the harness would get in a terrible mess. No, I reckon it's reindeer or nothing.

What bliss, though, to be comfortably fur-snuggled (or synthetic nylon-snuggled if you'd rather) as you skim above houses and hills with your luggage all round you. Lots of it. No struggling with the ritual humiliations inflicted by Ryanair, no poking about on Internet timetables that want every detail of your journey before they will tell you if they fly at all. No Prestwick, no sitting on the slatted bench at Kilwinning station for two hours, waiting for the Ardrossan train. Just whistle up the dream-team and you're off.

My travels always start as a dream. It's probably the result of too much *Arabian Nights* as a child. Magic carpets, djinns, flying horses – why aren't these things real? I want to be in wonderful places with incomprehensible languages going on and exotic clothes all round, while the smell of spicy food drifts through the warm air on a cloud of music on wailing pipes and little hand drums. No, honestly, such places do exist. It's just that getting to them involves going through the dreaded transport factory. Buy your virtual ticket on line, convert it into something tangible at the machine in the terminal, follow the instructions on the screen, do not attempt to think.

Nostalgia comes smiling in. She's a false jade, of course – it wasn't always splendid journeys on ships that provided lovely food while riding a rough sea, followed by enjoyable hitch-hiking and arrival at Youth Hostels housed in crumbling chateaux. There were hours spent sweating across sweltering Italy on the corridor floor of a packed train. There were long afternoons in the rain in some God-forsaken place in rural Austria. Steam trains, though glorious, gave you painful smuts in the eyes, specially if you hung out of the window. But these things were very real. Even if nasty, they had flavour.

That's why I want my reindeer. Unicorns would be better, but they might prove too mythical for any practical use. The idea of being free to go wherever you like, without pre-arrangement, is deeply seductive. Coming as I do from a wandering family with a habit of vanishing into foreign parts without trace, accountability still seems a bit of a bore. A small aeroplane would be nice if reindeer don't pass the reality test, but then there's the greenhouse gas. And getting a pilot's licence, not to speak of all the money involved.

Aeroplanes do have a certain mechanical enchantment, though. Little ones are charming, like flying VW Beetles. Even the big ones have something about them, once off the ground. I find it a great pleasure to watch the dipping of a wing as the horizon tilts and slides away. I love the gimcrack workings of all those little flaps – there's something so paper-dart about them, so implausibly simple. They look capable of failing at any minute, though they probably won't. The truth is, I am at my happiest in a state of slight danger. If things get too safe and boring, the impulse to nudge them along towards the interesting edge of the unknown is irresistible.

Hence the reindeer, you see. As the world becomes relentlessly safer, I claim my right to be reckless, at least in my dreams. The worst that can happen is death, and that's OK. But as I fly away through that unknown sky behind the magic team, I would like the experience to be astonishing and full of new interest.